C000214860

OREP
EDITIONS

Zone tertiaire de Nonant - 14400 BAYEUX
Tel: 02 31 51 81 31 - Fax: 02 31 51 81 32
info@orepeditions.com - **www.orepeditions.com**

Editor: Grégory Pique
Graphic design: Éditions OREP - **Layout:** Sophie Youf
English translation: Heather Inglis

ISBN: 978-2-8151-0106-6 – © Éditions OREP 2012

SWORD *BEACH*

Lord Lovat's piper Bill Millin preparing to land on Sword Beach with his bagpipes, the drones of which can be seen in front of his face. © *IWM B 5103.*

Everyone was behaving normally, I mean checking their kit, putting their kit on... I didn't think of being shot, how many Germans there, what was there, whether the smell of feeling of seasickness was still on me. We all got up on deck and we stood in the freezing wind watching the shoreline. Then the order came to get ashore, and I was very pleased to get ashore and no one was shouting that they were afraid or shouting that they were going to kill all these Germans. All people wanted really was to get off.

Lord Lovat was in the next ramp. There were two ramps at the front of the landing craft. I was up on one and he was up on this one. He jumped into the water. So I waited till he got in, because he was over six feet tall, to see what depth it was, and someone came up on to his empty ramp. Well, he was immediately shot. A piece of shrapnel or a bullet in the face and he fell and sank. Well, I jumped in pretty smart then. My kilt floated to the surface and the shock of the freezing cold water knocked all feelings of sickness from me and I felt great. I was so relieved of getting off that boat after all night being violently sick. I struck up the Pipes and paddled through the surf playing *Hieland Laddie*, and Lord Lovat turned round and looked at me and [gestured approvingly].

When I finished, Lovat asked for another tune. Well, when I looked round – the noise and people lying about shouting and the smoke, the crump of mortars, I said to myself, 'Well, you must be joking surely.'

He said, 'What was that? Would you mind giving us a tune?'

'Well, what tune would you like, Sir?'

'How about *The Road to the Isles*?'

'Now, would you want me to walk up and down, Sir?'

'Yes That would be nice. Yes, walk up and down.'

Bill Millin, Lord Lovat's piper

CONFRONTATION BETWEEN FOUR DIVISIONS ON THE BANKS OF THE ORNE

THE LANDING SITE

Four years, almost to the day, prior to the Normandy Landings, the British troops accomplished the feat of escaping from the Dunkirk pocket. Although the British Prime Minister Winston declared, 'You do not win wars with evacuations,' the experience was nevertheless to enable his country to re-form its army and to envisage a return to the Continent. But in the meantime, Churchill, who was well aware that it was impossible to attack the German forces head on, set to organising small-scale operations that were to sow an incessant sense of insecurity along the entire Atlantic coastline. These commando operations were of a totally new order for they required perfect coordination between the various army corps: the air, naval and land forces. Never before had the three military constituents worked together and, for that reason, it is most likely that these commando operations provided valuable lessons that were to contribute towards the success of the Normandy Landings.

Although very much alone for a year, Great Britain was finally to join forces with two critical allies: the Soviet Union following the launch of operation Barbarossa on the 22nd of June 1941, and the United States, after the Japanese bomber attack on Pearl Harbor on the 7th of December 1941. A landing operation was now feasible. As early as late December of the same year, during the Washington conference, the Americans and the British powers set their priority on crushing Nazi Germany: via the adoption of the Germany First strategy. However, over the coming months, Allied strategies were to diverge. The Americans were in favour of a direct attack on the German forces, preferably in France. Projects were therefore developed by the American military staff, such as operation Round Up, which planned for a landing operation in 1943 between Boulogne and Le Havre, and the Sledgehammer plan which targeted the Cotentin peninsula.

HOLDING THE LINE !

British propaganda poster illustrating Churchill's 'bulldog' tenacity. The British Prime Minister was behind the creation of the commando units that relentlessly intimidated the German defences as from 1940. © Jean Quellien

1944 YEAR OF DECISION "The supreme effort has still to be made". Rt. Hon. W. L. Mackenzie King

Canadian propaganda poster. 1944 was, indeed, a decisive year in the war, thanks to the success of the Allied landings in the West and the arrival of Soviet troops on the frontiers of the Riech. © Jean Quellien

The British command was far from approving these projects for one simple reason: it believed that a large-scale operation in France was, as yet, manifestly premature. The forces at the time being assembled in England needed to be considerably reinforced before embarking on any such landing operation. Meanwhile, peripheral operations could be launched in the Mediterranean. This was in line with Churchill's strategic aims of forestalling the Soviets in the Balkans and in Central Europe.

Hence, on the 8th of November 1942, the American forces landed in North Africa (operation Torch). They advanced laboriously towards Tunisia where they joined forces with General Montgomery's 8th Army, which had hounded Rommel's troops out of Egypt. After five months of resistance, the Axis forces finally surrendered at Bizerte early May 1943. The Allies could then continue their amphibious operations, landing first of all in Sicily, then in Italy where the German troops took advantage of favourable terrain. Late 1943, Churchill's plans for the Balkans had come to a standstill.

Meanwhile, the inter-Allied staff, the COSSAC (Chief of Staff to Supreme Allied Commander) was created in April 1943, in order to perfect the plans for the French landings. The task it faced was immense. It ranged from creating a significant number of landing barges to developing deception operations aimed at deluding the enemy as to the precise landing zone. Its commander, General Morgan, presented the committee's plans at the Quebec Conference, codenamed Quadrant, in August. Both Roosevelt and Churchill approved them. Operation Overlord was to be launched in Normandy in May 1944.

TWO DIVISIONS TO COVER THE EAST FLANK OF THE LANDING ZONE

The COSSAC was replaced by the SHAEF (Supreme Headquarters Allied Expeditionary Force) late 1943. This inter-Allied staff adopted and further improved the plans developed by General Morgan's team. General Eisenhower, commander of the SHAEF, along with the commander of ground forces, General Montgomery, realised that the COSSAC had targeted a far too narrow assault zone and an insufficient assault force to break through the German defence system. Furthermore, command of logistics was one of the keys to the landing operation's success. The Allies would need to rapidly take control of a port area, even if the construction of artificial harbours was already scheduled. Consequently, a new landing beach was considered to the south of the Cotentin peninsula, to enable the American troops who were to land there to rapidly take over the port of Cherbourg. Hence, the number of beaches was increased to five and the number of divisions from four (three infantry divisions and one airborne division) to eight (five infantry divisions and three airborne divisions).

In order to cover the east flank of the landing zone, they planned to drop the 6th Airborne Division between the Rivers Orne and Dives and to land the British 3rd Infantry Division on the beach codenamed Sword, stretching from Langrune-sur-Mer to Ouistreham. As from February 1944, both divisions began training exercises aimed at enabling them to accomplish, as best they could, their respective missions.

General Gale's paratroopers were to jump during the night of the 5th to the 6th of June and to secure the zone to the east of the River Orne. They were entrusted with a number of tasks. An airborne operation was planned, aimed at taking by surprise the bridges over the Orne and its canal between Bénouville and Ranville. Both bridges were essential for transferring reinforcements to support the troops dropped on the east bank of the river. The aim was consequently to take control of them without opposition. Conversely, five bridges over the Dives were to be destroyed to prevent German reinforcements from being rapidly brought in from the east. Finally, Lieutenant-Colonel Otway's 9th Battalion was to neutralise the Merville artillery battery, which was a considerable threat to troops landing on Sword Beach. Training was as intensive as military training can be. Replicas of the Bénouville and Ranville bridges and of the Merville battery were even built in order to optimise assault tactics.

Insignia of the two British divisions that were to fight along the banks of the River Orne: the 3rd Division's triangle, drawn by Montgomery himself when he was in command of the unit in 1940, and Bellerophon riding Pegasus, the paratroopers' emblem.

AIRBORNE

THE *1ER BFMC (BATAILLON DE FUSILIERS MARINS COMMANDOS)*

When France was defeated in 1940, Churchill ordered for the creation of a commando force aimed at harrassing the German troops along the Atlantic coast. Impressed by earlier raids, *Enseigne de Vaisseau* Philippe Kieffer - who had joined the Free French Forces in 1940 - decided to enlist in the British commandos. In the spring of 1942, 29 French soldiers trained at the Achnacarry Castle training centre in Scotland. Lost amidst the Scottish Highlands, the site was perfectly adapted for the future commandos' gruelling and highly selective preparation. These French troops were the first foreign contingent to be trained at Achnacarry. They were later joined by the Polish, Belgian, Norwegian and Dutch soldiers that comprised the No. 10 Inter-Allied Commando.

Before landing in Normandy, the French commandos took part in a range of different operations, under British command. Fifteen men in particular were among the forces that landed in Dieppe on the 19th of August 1942. In August 1943, the *1er Bataillon de Fusiliers Marins Commandos* was comprised of three troops - No. 1, No. 8 and a K-Gun support troop armed with Vickers machine guns.

After landing on Sword Beach, Kieffer's commandos joined the British paratroops in Amfreville on the evening of the 6th of June. A quarter of the men were lost - killed or wounded - and Kieffer himself had been hit twice.

The battalion then suffered two months of bitter combat before taking part in Operation Paddle, launched on the 16th of August, which marked the advance towards the Seine. Beuzeville was reached on the 23rd. The commandos were sent back to England the following day. Only 24 of the initial 177 troops survived the operation unscathed.

In turn, the 3rd Division's infantrymen were also hard at work. In coordination with naval forces, General Rennie's troops organised amphibious exercises in south Hampshire. They also meticulously studied the German defences and the topography of Sword Beach. The zone, stretching from Langrune-sur-Mer to Ouistreham, had been divided into four sectors, organised in alphabetical order: Oboe, Peter, Queen and Roger. However, all sectors were not to be used as landing zones, for there were large sandbanks off Lion-sur-Mer likely to cause landing barges to ground. Similarly, substantial German defences had been edified in the resort area of Ouistreham, known as Riva-Bella, and a frontal attack was unwise. Consequently, only the Queen sector, near La Brèche d'Hermanville, was to be used for landing troops. The resulting limited landing zone meant that only two battalions were to land during the first wave of assault, concurrent to four similar units on Juno and Gold.

British 3rd Infantry Division
(Major General Rennie) 25,000 men

8th Brigade (Brig. Cass) 1st wave of assault	185th Brigade (Brig. Smith) 2nd wave of assault	9th Brigade (Brig. Cunningham) 3rd wave of assault	Divisional Units
1st Btn, The South Lancashire Regiment (Lt. Col. Burbury)	**2nd Btn, The King's Shropshire Light Infantry** (Lt. Col. Maurice)	**2nd Btn, The Lincolnshire Regiment** (Lt. Col. Welby-Everard)	**3 artillery groups:** 7th Field Regiment RA, 33rd Field Regiment RA, 76th Field Regiment RA, (72 pieces of artillery) **1 anti-tank group:** 20th Anti-Tank Regiment RA (48 anti-tank guns)
2nd Btn, The East Yorkshire Regiment (Lt. Col. Hutchinson)	**2nd Btn, The Royal Warwickshire Regiment** (Lt. Col. Herdon)	**1st Btn, The King's Own Scottish Borderers** (Lt. Col. Renny)	**1 anti-aircraft group:** 92nd Light Anti-Aircraft, Regiment RA (54 x Bofors 40mm guns)
1st Btn, The Suffolk Regiment (Lt. Col. Goodwin)	**1st Btn, The Royal Norfolk Regiment** (Lt. Col. Bellamy)	**2nd Btn, The Royal Ulster Rifles** (Lt. Col. Harris)	**1 machine gun battalion:** (2nd Btn, The Middlesex Regiment MG) **1 reconnaissance unit:** 3rd Recce Regiment Northumberland Fusiliers

A further particularity of the Sword sector lay in the fact that the German strongpoints had been built, not only on the beach, but also further inland. They would therefore need to be weakened before 2nd and 3rd echelon troops could advance towards the 3rd Division's priority target: the town of Caen. Finally, five commando units were to reinforce General Rennie's division. Their mission consisted in weakening the defences at Riva-Bella before linking with and lending a hand to the paratroops to the east of the Orne.

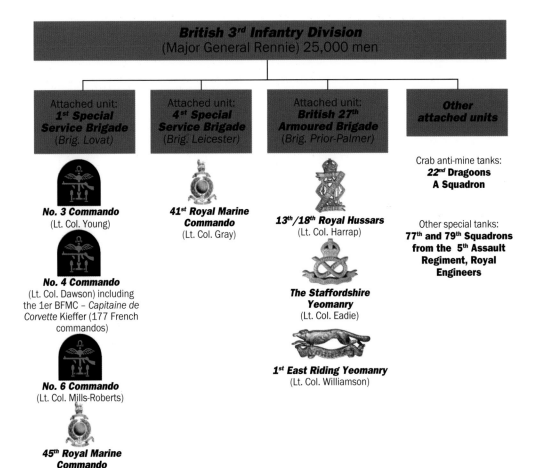

British 3rd Infantry Division
(Major General Rennie) 25,000 men

Attached unit:
1st Special Service Brigade
(Brig. Lovat)

Attached unit:
4st Special Service Brigade
(Brig. Leicester)

Attached unit:
British 27th Armoured Brigade
(Brig. Prior-Palmer)

Other attached units

No. 3 Commando
(Lt. Col. Young)

No. 4 Commando
(Lt. Col. Dawson) including the 1er BFMC – *Capitaine de Corvette* Kieffer (177 French commandos)

No. 6 Commando
(Lt. Col. Mills-Roberts)

45th Royal Marine Commando
(Lt. Col. Ries)

41st Royal Marine Commando
(Lt. Col. Gray)

13th/18th Royal Hussars
(Lt. Col. Harrap)

The Staffordshire Yeomanry
(Lt. Col. Eadie)

1st East Riding Yeomanry
(Lt. Col. Williamson)

Crab anti-mine tanks:
22nd Dragoons A Squadron

Other special tanks:
77th and 79th Squadrons from the 5th Assault Regiment, Royal Engineers

Lord Lovat

Lord Lovat, a 33 year-old Scot, was the latest in a long line of lords whose ancestors had arrived in Britain along with the Normans in the 11th century. Like many a loyal Scot, he was also one of a clan, the Frasers, of which he became the 25th chief upon the death of his father in 1933.

An officer in the Scots Guards, he was quick to volunteer for commando training. In command of unit No. 4, he took part in the raid on the Lofoten Islands in March 1941, then in the Dieppe landings in August 1942. Although the operation failed, his unit was the only one to have accomplished its mission - to neutralise the Hess battery in Varengeville.

Shortly before D-Day, he was entrusted with the command of the 1st Special Service Brigade reuniting four land-based commandos. In the company of his famous bagpipe player, Bill Millin, he landed on Sword Beach at 08:40. His brigade reached its target, Bénouville bridge, at midday and set up camp south of Sallenelles.

Lord Lovat was wounded on the 12th of June and was repatriated to Britain. Appointed Secretary of State for Foreign Affairs in 1945 under Churchill's government, he then travelled to the Soviet Union. He died in 1995 at the age of 84.

Lord Lovat. © *Life*

THE ATLANTIC WALL TO THE NORTH OF CAEN

On the 23rd of March 1942, Hitler issued a directive that was to lead to the birth of the Atlantic Wall, a line of defensive structures stretching from Norway to the Bay of Biscay and aimed at warding off Allied attacks. The Todt Organisation, a paramilitary organisation in charge of the construction of German fortifications, actively set to work. The German high command, the OKW, very quickly came to the conclusion that the landing operation would target northern France, in a zone where the English Channel of-

Construction of the Atlantic Wall not only occupied foreign manpower but also many local labourers.© *Bundesarchiv*

fered the shortest crossing. Fortifications were consequently largely concentrated in this sector, all the more so thanks to Allied disinformation campaigns, such as operation Fortitude, which further endorsed the Germans' miscalculation.

Late 1943, Field Marshal Rommel was appointed inspector of coastal defences. He engaged all his efforts and energy into improving the Atlantic Wall which, he was quick to realise, was far from the impenetrable barrier portrayed by German propaganda.

First of all, he had the beach covered with a series of obstacles that were completely concealed at high tide. As such, when the landing barges finally arrived - and he was convinced they would do so at high tide in order to reduce the distance the infantrymen would need to cover across the beach - they would be damaged or destroyed.

Rommel then intensified the number of *Wiederstandtnesten* (WN), the strongpoints that were dotted along the shoreline and equipped with machine guns, mortars and antitank guns to prevent troops from landing. Finally, he regularly inspected and accelerated the construction of coastal artillery batteries located further inland. Thanks to their powerful guns, these batteries were intended to destroy any Allied ships observed out in the high seas.

However, Rommel was convinced that all these fortifications were but a delusion. The Allied powers would eventually succeed in breaking through them. He believed, however, that these defences would sufficiently delay the landings to enable German armoured divisions to intervene and to permanently fend off any troops who had succeeded in landing. He was counting on bringing the Western Front's ten *Panzerdivisionen* as close as possible to the beaches. Rommel's superior, Field Marshal von Runstedt, and the commander of western armoured units, General von Schweppenburg, were totally opposed to this strategy. On the contrary, they planned to position armoured units further inland and to launch a powerful counter-attack after the Allies had effectively landed. Yet Rommel was sure that such an option was to be excluded; the Allied aviation was sure to thwart any attempts by the Panzer units to manoeuvre or to reassemble. And he proved to be right. Hitler was finally to bring the debate to a consensual close: certain divisions were to be posted near the beaches, the *21.Panzer* for example, whereas others were to be positioned further inland, such as the *12.SS Hitlerjugend* in Lisieux and the *Panzer-Lehr* in Chartres.

Although the extreme north of France was heavily defended, Normandy had not for as much been neglected. Rommel had fully grasped the weakness of defences in the sector, which he had reinforced, in particular via the presence of an armoured division to the south of Caen: the *21.Panzer*.

13

View of Sword Beach in February 1944. © *Bundesarchiv*

Hence, the paratroopers from the 6th Airborne Division and the infantrymen from the 3rd Division, would need to defy units from General Richter's *716.Infanterie-Division*, in particular units from his 736th Regiment, posted as follows:

LOCATION	STRONG POINT (code-name)	WEAPONS	COMPANY
Lion-sur-Mer	WN 21 (Trout)	2 x 50mm guns housed in casemates	10th company
La Brèche d'Hermanville	WN 20 (Cod)	1 x 88mm gun housed in a casemate 3 x 50mm guns, 2 of them in casemates	
Colleville-sur-Orne	WN 19	Troop quarters	4th company
Colleville-sur-Orne	WN 17 (Hillman)	Machine guns 736th Regiment Command post	
Colleville-sur-Orne artillery battery	WN 16 (Morris)	4 x 100mm Czech guns housed	
Saint-Aubin-d'Arquenay	WN 15 WN 15a	Troop quarters (WN 8 guns were stored here)	
Ouistreham (Southwest)	WN 14 (Sole)	Machine guns, 1st Battalion (736th Regiment) command post	
Ouistreham - 'Water Tower' artillery battery	WN 12 (Daimler)	4 x French 155mm guns housed in casemates	
Ouistreham (Southwest)	WN 11	Machine guns	
Riva-Bella	WN 10	1 x 75mm gun housed in a casemate 1 x 50mm gun housed in a casemate	2nd company
Ouistreham (south of the village)	WN 9	Machine guns	
Riva-Bella	WN 8	6 French 155mm guns in open gun emplacements	
		1 x 75mm gun housed in a casemate 1 anti-tank gun under the casino 2 x 50mm guns, 1 of them in a casemate	

A French 155mm gun, seized by the Germans and installed with five other guns in WN 8 at Riva-Bella. This picture clearly illustrates how vulnerable these open-air emplacements were to Allied bombardments. © Bundesarchiv

General Feuchtinger's *21.Panzer-division*, whose command post had been established in Saint-Pierre-sur-Dives, was also ready to intervene the very day of any Allied attack. The division, with its seventeen thousand men and its hundred armoured vehicles, was perfectly capable of repelling the assault on Sword Beach. Yet on the 5th of June, Feuchtinger was with his mistress in Paris, a rendezvous that was to generate a series of orders and counter orders throughout the morning of the 6th. Despite his friendship with Hitler, it was to cost him the court martial in March 1945.

The Flame Monument was erected on top of a German armoured cloche. It reminds us of the sacrifice paid by the first French troops to land on the 6th of June - Commandant Kieffer's commandos. The granite headstones in the foreground bear the names of those killed on the beach. © Jean Quellien

TARGET CAEN

THE PARACHUTISTS JUMP BY NIGHT

As the Allied ships approached the Normandy coastline, the first 6th Airborne units took off from England. After the pathfinders, whose mission was to mark out the drop zones, the first troops to set foot on Norman soil arrived aboard Major Howard's gliders. Their mission was crucial. They were to take control of two bridges over the Orne and its canal, for they were the only crossing points to the north of Caen. If captured intact, they would provide a unique link between the forces landed on Sword and the parachutists dropped between the Orne and the Dives.

Pegasus Bridge today. The original bridge was dismantled in 1993 during work to enlarge the canal; it was moved to the Memorial Pegasus park just a few metres away. © *Rights reserved*

At 00:16, the first glider violently touched ground just 50 metres from Bénouville bridge - a tremendous feat for its pilot. Howard's men quickly gathered their wits and rushed towards the bridge defences, to immediately neutralise them. They took the Germans totally by surprise. Two other gliders arrived a few minutes later, their crews offering precious support to those already on the ground. The bridge was taken - intact - in just five minutes. The sappers were delighted to discover that the demolition explosives were not in place.

Two other gliders had landed near Ranville bridge, 400 metres away. It was also effortlessly secured. However, one glider was missing. Its pilot had mistaken the Dives and the Orne and had landed thirteen kilometres away.

But this extraordinary surprise attack was a total success. Howard could now send the coded message 'Ham and Jam' to inform his superiors that his mission had been accomplished. Two hours later, reinforcements in the form of the 5th Parachute Brigade were dropped north of Ranville. Howard was now in a position to challenge any German counter-attacks.

Major Howard's Horsa gliders succeeded in landing barely a few metres from the bridge. The Café Gondrée can be seen

© IWM HO39183.

Further east, the 9th Battalion's mission was far less fortunate. Within two hours, of Lieutenant-Colonel Otway's initial 750 man-strong battalion, only 150 were still fit for combat and all of his heavy equipment had been lost. He nevertheless decided to pursue his mission - to neutralise the Merville battery, the guns of which were a serious threat for Sword Beach. At 04:30, the assault was launched. A deadly assault. Despite the loss of half of the unit, the battery was captured and its guns - of lower calibre than expected - were destroyed. Otway then retreated towards Amfreville.

The remaining men from the 3rd Brigade (Canadian 1st Battalion and British 8th Battalion) were entrusted with destroying the bridges over the Dives and the Divette to stop any German reinforcements in their tracks. Despite a scattered drop, the paratroops managed to destroy all five bridges.

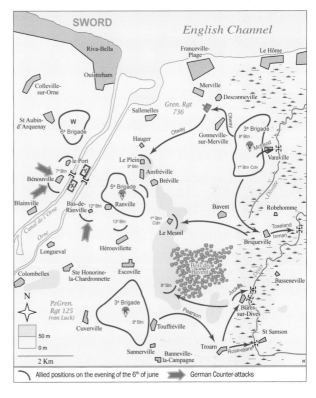

SWORD

English Channel

Riva-Bella
Franceville-Plage
Le Hôme
Ouistreham
Colleville-sur-Orne
Merville
Descanneville
St Aubin-d'Arquenay
W
6e Brigade
Sallenelles
Gren. Rgt 736
Otway
3e Brigade
9e Btn
McLeod
Hauger
Otway
Gonneville-sur-Merville
Varaville
le Port
Le Plein
9e Btn
1er Btn Cdn
7e Btn
Amfréville
Bénouville
5e Brigade
Bréville
Blainville
Bas-de-Ranville
12e Btn
Ranville
Bavent
Robehomme
Canal de l'Orne
13e Btn
1er Btn Cdn
Toseland
Orne
Le Mesnil
Inman
Longueval
Hérouvillette
Briqueville
Colombelles
Ste Honorine-la-Chardronnette
Escoville
Bois de Bavent
Basseneville
8e Btn
Juckes
N
PzGren. Rgt 125 (von Luck)
3e Brigade
Pearson
Bures-sur-Dives
Cuverville
8e Btn
Touffréville
St Samson
50 m
0 m
Sannerville
Banneville-la-Campagne
Troarn
Roseveare
2 Km
M

Allied positions on the evening of the 6th of june   German Counter-attacks

Two paratroopers guarding the road that leads to Bénouville. The German signposts are still in place. © IWM B 5291

By dawn, General Gale, commander of the 6th Airborne Division, was rightly satisfied. All his division's missions had been successfully accomplished; however at a loss of a thousand men, 600 of whom were unaccounted for. It later transpired that most of them were simply lost after the drop. They eventually caught up with their respective units over the following days.

Aerial view of Pegasus Bridge which crosses the canal that links the town of Caen with the sea and runs parallel to the River Orne.

The Café Gondrée is a site not to be missed for all 6th Airborne Division veterans. Every year, on the night of the 5th to the 6th of June, Major Howard's great feat is celebrated. © Mémorial de Caen

Pegasus Bridge

This drawbridge over the Caen canal was erected in 1935 to enable the canal to be crossed downstream of Normandy's capital town. In 1944, two cafés were located nearby, including the one held by the Gondrée family and welcoming, among other customers, the boatmen who worked along the canal. Shortly after midnight, the couple and their three daughters were liberated by Major Howard's men, whose blackened faces did little to reassure the children.

Since that memorable night, the café has become a key heritage site for veterans and their families. The drawbridge was rapidly renamed Pegasus Bridge in honour of the British parachutists whose emblem is the winged horse Pegasus. When the canal was enlarged in 1993, the bridge was rebuilt in the form of a larger-scale copy of the original, which now stands proud in the Memorial Pegasus park in Ranville.

Men from the 3rd Division's 1st South Lancashires crossing Pegasus Bridge the day after D-Day. © IWM

First attempt at designing an amphibious tank: this Valentine was surrounded by an inflatable skirt which enabled it to float. However, the skirt totally concealed its gun. © IWM

LANDING OF THE 3RD DIVISION

When the first parachute units took to the air, the Allied fleet had already left its home ports 24 hours ago. It was already approaching the Normandy coast via ten channels previously cleared by minesweepers. The ships comprising Force S, commanded by Rear Admiral Talbot, dropped anchor. They were backed up by several warships entrusted with the mission of covering the fleet's east flank from potential attacks by the *Kriegsmarine* units based in Le Havre. A total of two battleships, six cruisers and thirteen destroyers ensured this protection in the form of the bombardment Task Force D. At 05:30, the huge 381mm and 152mm guns opened fire on the German coastal artillery batteries from Colleville-sur-Orne (today called Colleville-Montgomery) to Villerville.

SHIPS	PRINCIPAL WEAPONS	TARGET
HMS Ramillies	8 x 381mm guns 12 x 152mm guns	Mont-Canisy artillery battery (Bénerville-sur-Mer)
HMS Warspite	8 x 381mm guns 10 x 152mm guns	Villerville artillery battery
HMS Arethusa	6 x 152mm guns	Merville artillery battery Mont des Grangues artillery battery
HMS Danae	5 x 152mm guns	'Water Tower' artillery battery in Ouistreham
ORP Dragon Polish cruiser	5 x 152mm guns	Colleville-sur-Orne artillery battery
HMS Frobisher	7 x 190mm guns	Riva-Bella artillery battery
HMS Mauritius	12 x 152mm guns	Mont des Grangues artillery battery
HMS Roberts	2 x 381mm guns	Houlgate artillery battery

Men from the 45th Royal Marine Commando approaching Sword Beach. They were to join forces as quickly as possible with the parachutists in Bénouville.© IWM MH33547 ▶

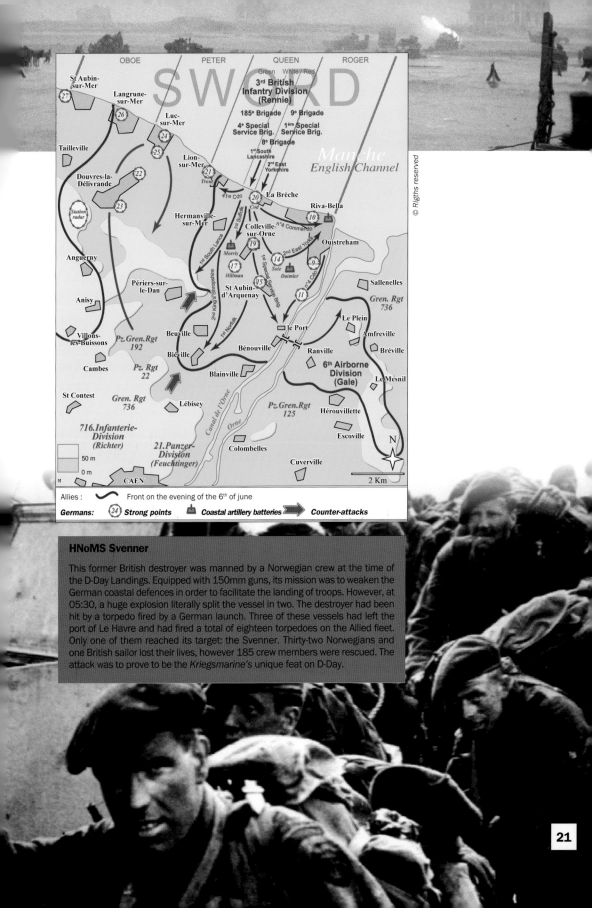

SWORD

OBOE	PETER	QUEEN	ROGER
		Green / White / Red	

3rd British Infantry Division (Rennie)

St Aubin-sur-Mer
27
Langrune-sur-Mer
26
Luc-sur-Mer
24
Tailleville
25
Lion-sur-Mer
21
Douvres-la-Délivrande
22
Station radar
23
Hermanville-sur-Mer
Anguerny
Périers-sur-le-Dan
Anisy
St Aubin-d'Arquenay
Villons-les-Buissons
Beuville
Cambes
Biéville
Pz. Rgt 22
St Contest
Gren. Rgt 736
Lébisey
Pz.Gren.Rgt 192
Blainville
716.Infanterie-Division (Richter)
21.Panzer-Division (Feuchtinger)
CAEN

185e Brigade   9e Brigade
4e Special Service Brig.   1ère Special Service Brig.
8e Brigade
1st South Lancashire
2nd East Yorkshire
41st Cdo
Troon
20
Cod
La Brèche
Riva-Bella
10
Colleville-sur-Orne   n°4 Commando
19
Morris
2nd East York
Ouistreham
17
Hillman
14
Sole
Daimler
9
15
1st Special Service Brig.
11
Sallenelles
Gren. Rgt 736
le Port
Le Plein
Amfreville
Bénouville
Ranville
Bréville
6th Airborne Division (Gale)
Le Mesnil
Pz.Gren.Rgt 125
Hérouvillette
Escoville
Colombelles
Cuverville

1st South Lanca
1st King's Shropshire
1st Norfolk
Canal de l'Orne
Orne

Manche
English Channel

N

Scale: 50 m / 0 m
2 Km

Allies: Front on the evening of the 6th of june
Germans: 24 Strong points   Coastal artillery batteries   Counter-attacks

HNoMS Svenner

This former British destroyer was manned by a Norwegian crew at the time of the D-Day Landings. Equipped with 150mm guns, its mission was to weaken the German coastal defences in order to facilitate the landing of troops. However, at 05:30, a huge explosion literally split the vessel in two. The destroyer had been hit by a torpedo fired by a German launch. Three of these vessels had left the port of Le Havre and had fired a total of eighteen torpedoes on the Allied fleet. Only one of them reached its target: the Svenner. Thirty-two Norwegians and one British sailor lost their lives, however 185 crew members were rescued. The attack was to prove to be the *Kriegsmarine's* unique feat on D-Day.

These special tanks have just reached the Queen sector opposite the German position codenamed Cod. © IWM B5111

Meanwhile, the 3rd Division infantrymen began their perilous transhipment by climbing down from their transport ships towards the LCA (Landing Craft Assault) landing barges that would take them to the beach. And they were not alone. Several amphibious assault ships, referred to as LCTs (Landing Craft Tanks) were also heading for the coast, boarded with Duplex Drive amphibious tanks, special tanks and Priest self-propelled guns.

Then liners, destroyers, rocket launcher barges and self-propelled guns took over and bombarded the German strong points.

Five kilometres from the shoreline, amphibious tanks were thrown into the choppy seas. Their pumps were rapidly activated for the heavy swell was washing over their inflatable skirts. Only thirty-four of a total of forty Sherman DDs actually reached the shore. At 07:25, the ramps were lowered and the men thrust forward.

Nervous gazes as the troops approach the beach. © IWM BU1191

Some of the first troops to be wounded receiving first aid in the shelter of a Churchill Petard armed with a 290mm mortar designed to weaken the German blockhouses. © IWM B5095

07:25 THE SOUTH LANCASHIRES ON QUEEN WHITE

The special tanks were the first to reach Sword Beach, just a few minutes before the infantrymen. The Crab tanks whipped up the sand with their flails to eliminate any mines, whilst the other armoured vehicles targeted the German casemates. Amidst the resulting battle, the men from the 1st South Lancashire's A Company landed in a defensive position codenamed Cod by the British and sustained heavy losses including their commander, Major Harwood. C Company arrived further west and was more fortunate. Yet the third company to land, B Company, also found itself immediately opposite Cod and suffered many losses. Major Harrison was killed almost instantly, as was the battalion's commander, Lieutenant-Colonel Burbury. Nevertheless, the South Lancs managed to bypass the casemate located furthest to the

Men from the 3rd Division seeking protection behind a vehicle in the Queen sector.
© IWM B5094

west and seized the German strongpoint from the rear. Backed by the East Yorkshires who had landed in the Queen Red sector, Cod was finally neutralised. At 09:00 hours, the battalion reached Hermanville where it entrenched itself, for German armoured vehicles thwarted any hopes of accessing the ridge at Périers.

07:25 THE EAST YORKSHIRES ON QUEEN RED

In the Queen Red sector, the East Yorkshires were also to fall victim to deadly gunfire from Cod. Rapidly, the dead and the wounded accumulated on the beach under showers of machine gun, mortar and anti-tank gunfire. A total of two hundred men were never to advance any further than the sandy shoreline, however Cod was soon to fall into British hands. An hour and a half after they had arrived, the East Yorks were in a position to advance inland towards two further strongpoints codenamed Sole and Daimler. Once more, violent combat broke out and the

Troops from the 3rd Division in front of the Hôtel de la Brèche, which still stands today, on the square in La Brèche d'Herman-ville. © IWM B5038

Germans only surrendered after several hours of hostilities. Lieutenant-Colonel Hutchison's men took control of Sole in the afternoon and the guns located at Daimler, in the vicinity of the Ouistreham water tower, were only neutralised after nightfall.

07:32 HONOUR TO THE FRENCH TROOPS

Commandant Kieffer's 177 French troops had the distinguished honour of being the first to set foot on Sword Beach. At 07:32, as LCIs 523 and 527 reached the shore, they were welcomed by enemy gunfire. The first soldiers fell. Others rushed to the dune, however, 40 of them were killed or wounded, including Kieffer himself. Rapidly bandaged, he resumed his commanding role. After leaving their packs amidst the ruins of a holiday camp, the commandos split into three troops (1st, 8th and K-Gun) and headed

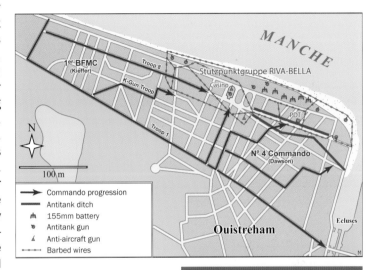

eastwards towards the fortified position around the Riva-Bella casino. By 09:00, the men had set to their task, but were struggling to reduce the enemy defences. The main road leading to the casino was blocked by an impassible chicane wall and the commandos became the target of a 20mm gun. Their attempts to reduce it to silence using a PIAT antitank rocket launcher failed. Further west, troop 8 was more successful and, with support from another 13th/18th Hussars tank rounded up by Kieffer, the casino position was finally neutralised. The commandos then returned to the holiday camp at 11:30, before heading for Bénouville. By the evening of the 6th of June, they had joined forces with the parachutists from the 9th Battalion in Amfreville. They took stock of their losses: 25% of the commando had been killed or wounded.

Capitaine de Corvette **Philippe Kieffer's** academic qualifications were far from predestining him for a military career. When the war broke out, his vocation was in finance. He volunteered for enlistment in the French Navy and was posted aboard the cruiser Courbet. When the armistice was signed, he headed for England and joined the Forces françaises libres (Free French Forces). Two years later, he was appointed in command of the first French commandos to be formed by the British, at the military training centre in Achnacarry. On D-Day, his men were offered the immense honour of being the first commandos to land; however, the Germans extended a merciless welcome and forty of Kieffer's one hundred and seventy-seven men were killed or wounded. Kieffer was himself wounded on two occasions. After the war, he resigned to embark on a political career. Philippe Kieffer died in 1962 and is laid to rest in Grandcamp-Maisy cemetery, in Calvados.

These Beach Group troops have just landed. They were in charge of clearing the beaches to facilitate landing conditions for those to

An LCI (Landing Craft Infantry) approaching Sword Beach. The shoreline is cluttered with special tanks. © IWM B005102.

08:00 ARRIVAL OF LORD LOVAT'S COMMANDOS

Further east, the rest of No. 4 Commando was concentrating its efforts on WN 8. The position was rapidly neutralised, however more intense combat was underway in the vicinity of the canal locks. Amidst the battle, the 17 metre-high tower that housed the German battery's firing command post was virtually ignored. Sappers were finally to blow up its main entrance and the garrison to surrender on the 9th of June. The remainder of Lord Lovat's brigade arrived at 08:30. To the sound of the bagpipes, played by his personal piper, Bill Millin, the Scottish officer immediately headed for Bénouville to join forces with the British paratroopers who had been bravely challenging German attacks since the previous night. At 12:00 hours, the men defending the bridges over the Orne and its canal could hear the melody played by Millin who was advancing with his bagpipes amidst the whistling bullets. The commandos and the paras were now reunited. Finally, troops from the 41st Royal Marine Commando landed at the extremity of the Queen White sector under bursts of German gunfire. Lieutenant-Colonel Gray divided his men into two groups and attacked the Trout strong point and the château in Lion-sur-Mer. He was then to join the commandos who had landed on Juno Beach. However, the Germans were perfectly entrenched in their positions and the green berets were insufficiently armed to dislodge them. They were only to take control of the German positions the next day, backed up by gunfire from the destroyers anchored offshore.

Men from the 41st Royal Marine Commando immediately after they landed on Sword - they grouped together to continue their progression towards WN 21 (Trout) in Lion-sur-Mer. It was to take them two days to finally overpower the strongpoint before joining their counterparts who had landed on Juno. © IWM B5090

CAEN STILL TO BE TAKEN

After the battalions that formed the first wave of assault, the 1st Suffolks arrived in turn around 09:00 hours. They advanced towards Colleville and set to weakening the defensive positions there, WN 16 and 17, codenamed Morris and Hillman by the Allies. WN 16 was an artillery battery comprised of four 100mm guns installed within casemates, and was protected by machine guns, barbed wire and minefields. Its garrison, essentially composed of Polish soldiers, had suffered greatly from the bombardments and was quick to surrender.

Hillman was another story. The site, protected by minefields, networks of barbed wire and machine gun shelters, was the headquarters of the German 716th Division's 736th Regiment. Its commander, Colonel Krug, had no intention of submitting to the Allied attack. Preceded by an artillery barrage, the assault was launched at 13:00. As the Royal Engineers intervened amidst the minefields and barbed wires, the men from A Company were hit by German machine gunfire, suffering heavy losses, including their captain, Ryley. Things barely improved after the arrival of tanks, incapable of breaking through the concrete shells. A second attack also failed. At 15:00, the 1st Norfolks, positioned nearby, also sustained terrible losses. At 17:00, after a third bombardment, five flail tanks drove through the minefields and the maze of barbed wire, followed by the infantry. The British troops secured their positions but it took a further three hours of combat to overwhelm the last pockets of resistance. Entrenched inside his blockhouse, Krug only surrendered at 06:45 the following day.

A Sherman Crab in action. The flails attached to a rotating cylinder were designed to set off the underground mines.

Infantrymen from the 8th Brigade advancing towards Caen, with support from 13th and 18th Royal Hussars tanks. © IWM B5091

Early in the afternoon, the 9th Brigade was the last to set foot on Sword Beach. The hold-up also hindered Brigadier Cunningham's men. He eventually sent his men towards Périers; they were later to reassemble with the Canadian troops who had landed on Juno Beach. However, on the outskirts of Hermanville, the British officer came across his superiors, General Rennie and General Crocker, respectively in command of the 3rd Division and I Corps. Faced with the incessant German attacks on the parachutists to the east of the Orne, Cunningham received orders to turn eastwards. Fatefully, before he could contact his various units, the commander of the 9th Brigade was wounded by a mortar shell and evacuated. Consequently, the bottleneck on the beach, the long and painstaking reduction of inland strongpoints, and the dispersal of the 9th Brigade were to combine to deprive the British troops of their key target: Caen.

The continuous influx of reinforcements and the narrowness of the village streets and roads leading to Caen led to several traffic jams throughout the entire day of the 6th of June. © IWM B5091

For indeed, hesitation on the British front was to allow the *21.Panzer* to establish positions to the north of the Norman capital. At 15:00 hours, the leading units from the 2nd King's Shropshire Light Infantry, who had reached Biéville and Beuville, found themselves face to face with Feuchtinger's *Panzergrenadiers* in the vicinity of the Lébisey woods. To the west, two *Kampfgruppen* (combat groups) had been formed and were advancing towards the coast. The Panzer Regiment's 22 tanks were the target of Allied anti-tank guns which succeeded in putting thirteen of them out of action. Conversely, units from the *Panzergrenadier Regiment 192* managed to make their way to the shoreline between Luc-sur-Mer and Lion-sur-Mer, from where they could admire the incredible sight of the Allied fleet that stretched out for miles before their very eyes. At 21:00 hours, above their heads, they could see the planes and gliders that were transporting men and supplies from the 6th Airborne Brigade, the last of General Gale's 6th Airborne Division units. Under the genuine threat of finding themselves surrounded, the *Panzergrenadiers* retreated under cover of darkness. The only notable counter-attack on the 6th of June had failed to throw the Allies back into the sea.

A self-propelled gun belonging to the *21.PanzerDivision*. The unit was equipped with a number of spoiled tanks, French in particular, upon which the Germans had installed their own guns. © *Calvados Departmental Archives*

On the evening of the 6th of June, 3rd Division artillerymen watching reinforcements from Gale's 6th Airborne Division arrive by glider. © *IWM B5046*

Emergency teams in action amidst the ruins of Caen after the bombardments on the 6th of June. © *Calvados Departmental Archives*

Hence, by the evening of D-Day, the British paratroopers and infantrymen had succeeded in establishing a solid bridgehead to the north of Caen, at a cost of six hundred losses for the 3rd Infantry Division and a thousand for the 6th Airborne Division. Although the landings had met with success, the British troops had not reached Caen. Before they could finally take control of the Norman capital, they were to endure four long weeks of combat and to sustain great losses. Perhaps a more vigorous attack on the Périers ridge could have limited such losses and the destruction of over 70% of the town.

Caen was among the towns that were bombarded during the Battle of Normandy - 75% of the town was destroyed and 2,000 civilians were killed. © *NARA* ▼

War memorial in honour of the 3rd Division, in Périers-sur-le-Dan. The village was only liberated on the 7th of June after the German retreat. They had succeeded in weaving their way between the British troops from Sword and the Canadians from Juno. © *ONAC Calvados.*

Caen – a bombed city

As were many other towns, Caen was the target of Allied fighter-bombers as from the 6th of June, their aim being to prevent German reinforcements from reaching the landing beaches. In the morning, planes tried in vain to destroy the four bridges over the Orne. By 13:30, total havoc reigned. Two hundred tonnes of bombs had set the entire Saint-Jean quarter ablaze. Surviving civilians took advantage of a calm spell to flee the town. Bombardments resumed in the evening. Three hundred civilians were killed and the bridges were still intact; elements from the *21.Panzer* even succeeded in advancing through the town to cut off access from the north. At 02:40, once more, the bombers discharged their merciless cargo. The population reassembled to the west of the town, within a refuge zone comprising the Men's Abbey and the Bon Sauveur hospital. Over ten thousand inhabitants took shelter within this genuine town within the town to which supplies were brought in by young emergency teams.

Civilians sought refuge in the Men's Abbey. They were to stay there until the town's north bank was liberated on the 9th of July. © IWM

On the evening of the 7th of June, ahead of operation Charnwood aimed at liberating the town, Caen's north quarters were, once again, reduced to dust and rubble by 2,300 tonnes of bombs. The Vaugueux, Saint-Julien and Gaillon quarters had ceased to exist. Two days later, Canadian and British troops nevertheless entered Caen and liberated the north bank of the River Orne. The south bank was to stay in enemy hands until the 19th of July, when the Canadians finally drove the Germans into retreat. A total of two thousand of Caen's inhabitants were killed during the five-week battle.

31

Three Canadians: Bernard Hoo, John MacCouville and J. R. Kostick from the Queen's Own Rifles of Canada posing in front of a signpost on the Bayeux road in Caen's Maladrerie quarter, on the afternoon of the 9th of July 1944. © *Canadian National Archives*

A magnificent restored Dakota welcomes visitors at the entrance to the Merville battery. © OREP

Steles have been erected on the very site where Major Howard's gliders landed on the night of the 5th to the 6th of June. © OREP

The Sword sector is home to a veritable wealth of commemorative sites. Bénouville and Ranville are among those not to be missed, with the famous Pegasus Bridge, Café Gondrée and Memorial Pegasus, a museum which retraces the paratroopers' steadfast commitment on that crucial night. Further north, the Merville artillery battery has been restored to offer a breathtaking insight into Otway's men's unique experience. A striking Dakota glider is on display at the museum entrance.

In Ouistreham, several monuments have been erected to commemorate the landing of Philippe Kieffer's 177 French commandos, including a small museum located just a few steps from the casino. Today, the immense seventeen metre-high tower still overlooks the resort of Riva-Bella and now houses a fascinating museum on the fortifications that comprised the Atlantic Wall.

The grounds of the Pegasus Memorial Museum. © Pegasus Memorial Museum